Alus, Ka, Kasar

or

Delicate, Or, Coarse

Buku 5

Book 5 - Antonyms

Chakapan Baba Ni Ari series

Baba Malay Today series

All Rights Reserved.
No part of this publication may be reproduced, stored in a retrieval system, or transmitted, in any form or by any means electronic, mechanical, photocopying, recording or otherwise, without the prior written permission of the publishers.

Theresa Fuller asserts the moral right to be identified as the author of this work.

Bare Bear Media

ISBN 978-1-925748-22-2 - Print
ISBN 978-1-925748-23-9 - Ebook

Cover by Helzkat Designs

Copyright March 2023©

Sincere thanks to my husband, Paul, who supported this work in every way possible. I love you.

National Library of Australia
US Library of Congress - TXu 2-377-446

Published 26th of June 2023

Introduction - Antonyms

Language is powerful.

In writing this text, I applied the SHOW don't TELL method. I wanted the reader to be able to pick up this book and begin to learn. Much as you would pick up a game and play.

> Chobak.
>
> To try.

Antonyms i.e., opposites are generally adjectives or adverbs, but they can also be nouns and verbs. Hence whatever rules apply to the usage of adjectives, adverbs, nouns and verbs, should also apply.

But really, use the language as much as you can and don't worry if you make mistakes, or break any rules. I have been told on good authority that every family uses Baba Malay a little differently.

The most important thing is to use it.

Please also note that from page 160 onwards I have tried to portray the average family structure but in reality there is no average family.

And I have included charts for the Pangkat Sedara i.e., Extended Family Members.

At the end of the day, have fun.

This is Baba Malay, the language of the Peranakans.

> **YOUR** language.

Baba Malay

Baba Malay is the language of my ancestors.

A language that I discovered late in 2021 was about to go extinct with fewer than a thousand speakers in the world. I took a course in Baba Malay taught by Kenneth Chan, author of *BABA MALAY FOR EVERYONE - A comprehensive guide to the Peranakan language.* This was my start to saving Baba Malay.

But I believed much more had to be done.

The book you hold in your hands is the result of my mad persistence to save my language. While there are books out there on Baba Malay, I found little in the way for children. As a teacher, I believe that to save a language we must start with the young.

I wanted a book that parents could give to their children.
One I could give to my kids.

This is my attempt.

Theresa, affectionately known in the Peranakan community as Bibek Theresa.

Sydney,
29th of May, 2022

Chobak

Chobak = To Try

I love Baba Malay.

Contents

Introduction	3
Baba Malay	4
Ya - Yes	8
Tak - No, Not	9
Tak'ah/Ta'ah - There is not	10
Takleh - Cannot, Not Possible	11
Chobak - Ya/Tak/Tak'ah/Takleh	12
Bukan - No, Not	13
List of Opposites - A & B	14
C, D & E	15
F, G & H	16
I, J, K & L	17
M, N & O	18
P, Q, R & S	19
T & W	20
Sample Sentences	21
My Family = Gua Mia Anak-Beranak	22
My Cousins = Gua Mia Piau	23
My Aunts & Uncles = Pangkat Sedara (Father)	24
My Aunts & Uncles = Pangkat Sedara (Mother)	25
My Grandparents = Pangkat Sedara (Father)	26
My Grandparents = Pangkat Sedara (Mother)	27
Extended Family Glossary	28
Notes	30
About the Author	31
More books in the Baba Malay Today Series	32

Gua sayang Chakapan Baba.

YA - Yes

Bus = Bair

Our first opposite is **'YA'** sometimes spelt as 'IA'. YA is an adverb that means 'Yes'.

Ya.
Yes.

Ya, bair ni pi Seletar.
Yes, this bus goes to Seletar.

Ya, saya dari Singapura.
Yes, I am from Singapore.

Lu tinggair kat Perth?
Do you live in Perth?

Ya, saya tinggair kat Perth.
Yes, I live in Perth.

Other forms of usage for Ya
Ya Jugak = Oh, yes!
Ya Tak Ya Pulak = So It Seems
Ya Ya Bukan = That Which is Untrue

TAK - No, Not

House = Rumah

'**TAK**' is an adverb that means 'No' or 'Not' and is derived from 'TIDAK'. While 'TAK' is used with verbs and adjectives.

Its two most common forms are:

Tak' ah or Ta'ah = There is not (See Page 148)
Takleh or Tak'leh = Cannot; Not Possible (See Page 149)

Tak can be used by itself.

Mary mana? Dia tak dalam rumah.
Where is Mary? She is not in the house.

Glossary
Ada = Have/Has

Other forms of usage for Tak
Tak'kan = As If; As Though (From Tidak Akan)
Takmo = Not Wanting (From Tidak Mahu)
Takpa = Never Mind; Not to Mind (From Tidak Apa)

Idiom - Tidak
Entah Padi Entah Dedak, Entah Jadi Entah Tidak = There's many a slip "twixt the cup and the lips."

TAK' AH/TA' AH - There is not

Grandfather = Kong Kong

"TAK' AH" or **"TA' AH"** is derived from 'TIDAK ADA.'

Ada = Verb meaning 'To Have'

Tak. Ta' ah. Tak' ah.
No. Do not have. Do not have.

Gua ada Kong Kong.
I have a grandfather.

Gua tidak ada Mama. Gua tak' ah Mama.
I do not have a grandmother.

Lu ada anjing? Gua tak' ah anjing. Tak' ah.
Do you have a dog? I do not have a dog. Do not have.

Gua ada tarok changkir kat atair piring.
I have put the cup on top of the plate.

Gua tak' ah tarok changkir kat atair piring.
I have not put the cup on top of the plate.

> Glossary
> Ada = To Have, Present, Existence
> Changkir = Cup
> Piring = Plate
> Tarok = Put or place

Gua mesti belajair Chakapan Baba.

TAKLEH - Cannot, Not Possible

Ball = Bola

'TAKLEH' is derived from 'TIDAK BOLEH.'

Boleh = Modal Verb used to express the ability or the permission to perform an activity

Gua boleh main bola.
I can play ball.

Gua takmo main bola.
I do not want to play ball.

Gua tak boleh main bola. Gua takleh main bola.
I cannot play ball. Or I am unable to play ball.

Saya boleh tarok mangkok kat bawah piso.
I can put the bowl under the knife.

Saya takleh tarok garfu di bawah mangkok.
I cannot put the fork under the bowl.

Glossary
Atair Loteng = Upstairs
Beli = Buy
Boleh = Can
Main = Play
Takleh = Cannot

CHOBAK - YA/TAK/TAK'AH/TAKLEH

Restaurant = Keday Makan

Select the correct word

Yes, I like to eat.
e.g. (**Ya**/Tak/Tak'ah/Takleh), gua suka makan.

1. Yes, I like going to the restaurant.
   (Ya/Tak/Tak'ah/Takleh), saya suka pi keday makan.

2. I have not gone over there.
   Saya (ya/tak/tak'ah/takleh) pi sana.

3. I cannot play ball.
   Gua (ya/tak/tak'ah/takleh) main bola.

4. Are you hungry? Yes.
   Lu lapair? (Ya/Tak/Tak'ah/Takleh).

5. Eh, did you make any cakes? I did not made any cakes because I cannot make cakes.
   Eh, lu ada bekin kueh? Gua (Ya/Tak/Tak'ah/Takleh) bekin kueh pasair gua (Ya/Tak/Tak'ah/Takleh) bekin kueh.

Answers: 1. Ya. 2. Tak or Tak'ah. 3. Takleh. 4. Ya. 5. Tak'ah. Takleh

BUKAN - No, Not

Grandmother = Mama

'BUKAN' means '**No**' or '**Not**.' Bukan tends to be used with nouns and pronouns.

Ni bukan gua mia Mama.
This is not my grandmother.

Lu orang Peranakan? Bukan, saya orang Italy.
Are you Peranakan? No, I am Italian.

Sapa makan semua kuch? Bukan, gua.
Who ate all the cakes? Not I.

Ni bukan gua mia bair. Ni bair tak pi Serangoon.
This is not my bus. This bus does not go to Serangoon.

Lu salah. Ni bair ada pi Serangoon.
You are wrong. This bus does go to Serangoon.

Takpa. Gua boleh jalan.
Never mind. I can walk.

Glossary
Bair = Bus
Jalan = Walk
Lapair = Hungry

List of Antonyms

A

A lot of = Banyak/Manyak
Able = Boleh
Afraid = Takot
Aged = Tua
Alone = Diri Seniri
Appropriate behaviour = Seronoh

Ask = Tanya

A little = Sikit
Unable = Tak Boleh or Takleh
Brave = Brani
Young = Mundah
Together = Sama Sekali
Inappropriate Behaviour
 = Tak Seronoh
Answer = Jawab

B

Bad = Jahat
Bad Luck = Tengkah Burok
Beautiful = Chantek
Behind = Belakang
Before = Belom
Big = Besair [Besar]
Black = Itam
Bottom = Bawah
Bright = Terang

Good = Baik
Good luck/lucky = Naseb Baik
Ugly = Burok
In Front = Depan
After = Lepair
Small = Kechik
White = Puteh
Top = Atair [Atas]
Dark = Gelap

NOTE: Words in brackets [ ] are the Kasar/Kasair version.

Which to use - jahat or nakair?
Jahat is pure malicious evil. However, nakair is more akin to mischievous.

C

Cheap = Murah
Child = Anak
Clean = Bersih
Clever = Panday
Close = Tutop
Coarse = Kasair [Kasar]
Cold = Sejok
Contented = Senang Ati
Correct = Betol

Expensive = Mahair [Mahal]
Adult = Orang Tua
Dirty = Kotor
Stupid = Bodoh
Open = Bukak
Delicate = Alus
Hot = Panair [Panas]
Discontented = Susah Ati
Wrong = Salah

D

Dark = Gelap
Dawn = Pagi
Death = Maot
Difficult = Susah
Diligent = Rajin
Dry = Kering

Bright = Terang
Twilight = Sinjakala
Life = Idop
Easy = Senang
Lazy = Malair [Malas]
Wet = Basah

E

Early = Siang
East = Timor
Easy = Senang
Easy Going = Chin Chai
Employer = Towkay
Employed = Kreja
Evil = Jahat

Late = Lambat
West = Barat
Hard = Susah
Fussy = Kewat
Employee = Orang Gaji
Unemployed = Tak Kreja
Good = Baik

Lu mo beljair Chakapan Baba.

F

Fall = Jatoh
Far = Jaoh
Fast = Chepat
Fat = Gemok
Few = Sikit
Find = Chari
Forget = Lupa
Friend = Kawan
Front = Depan

Rise = Naik
Near = Dekat
Slow = Pelan-Pelan
Thin = Kurus
Many = Banyak/Manyak
Lose = Ilang
Remember = Ingat
Enemy = Musoh
Back = Belakang

G

Generous = Murah Ati
Gentle = Lemah-lembut
Giant = Gergasi, Jin
Give = Kasih
Good = Baik

Stingy = Kedekut
Rude = Bo Ka Si, Cho Lo
Tiny = Kechik
Receive = Dapat, Terima
Bad = Jahat or
Naughty = Nakair [Nakal]

H

Happy = Senang Ati, Cheng Ati
Hard = Kuat
He = Dia
Head = Kepala
Heaven = Shorga
Here = Sini
Hello = Apa Khabar

Unhappy = Kek Sim
Soft = Lembek
She = Dia
Backside = Pantat
Hell = Noraka
There = Sana
Goodbye = Selamat Tinggair or Selamat Jalan (depending on whether you are leaving or going)

I

Important (person) = Iau Kin
Increase (in price) = Naik Harga
Instructor = Guru
Into = Masok

Nobody = Tak Sapa
Decrease = Turun Harga
Student = Murid
Out of = Keluair

J

Joy = Hoa Hi
Junior = Bawah Tangan
(assistant to a senior)

Grief = Sedeh Ati
Senior = Inche

K

Kind = Ati Baik
King = Raja

Cruel = Tak Ati Baik
Queen = Raja Prompuan

L

Laugh = Kertawa
Left = Kiri
Live = Rezeki
Long = Panjang
Love = Sayang
Low = Rendah

Cry = Nangis
Right = Kanan
Die = Mati
Short = Pendek
Hate = Benchi
High = Tinggi

M

Male = Jantan
Marry = Kahwen
Messy = Semak
More = Lagik

Female = Prompuan
Divorce = Cheray
Neat = Kemas
Less = Kurang

N

Narrow = Sempet
Near = Dekat
New = Baru
Night = Malam
Noisy = Bising
Now = Sekarang
North = Utara

Wide = Lebair
Far = Jaoh
Old = Tua
Day = Ari
Quiet = Diam
Then = Dulu
South = Selatan

O

Obedient = Kuai
Old = Tua
Open = Bukak
Over Here = Sebelah Sini

Disobedient = Jahat or Nakair
Young = Mundah
Shut = Tutop
Over There = Sebelah Sana

P

Patient = Sabair
Polite = Tau Adat
Poor = Miskin
Pretty = Chantek
Prince = Anak Raja
Crown Prince = Raja Mundah
Proud = Lawa
Pure = Jernih

Impatient = Tak Sabair
Rude = Kurang Ajair
Rich = Kaya
Ugly = Burok
Princess = Peteri

Demure = Lau Sit
Impure = Tak Jernih

Q

Quickly = Lekair-lekair

Slowly = Pelan-Pelan

R

Start of the Road = Kepala Jalan

End of the Road = Buntot Jalan

S

Salt = Garam
Short = Pendek
Shy = Malu
Skinny = Kurus Kering
Son = Anak Jantan
Start = Mulai
Straight (Hair) = Tak Keriting

Sugar = Gula
Tall = Tinggi
Not shy = Tak Malu
Fat = Gemok
Daughter = Anak Prompuan
Stop = Brenti
Curly = Keriting

T

Take = Ambek
Tasty = Sedap
This = Ini or Ni
Tomorrow = Besok

Give = Kasih
Tasteless = Tawair
That = Itu or Tu
Yesterday = Semalam

W

War = Perang
Weather = Cuacha :
(Clear Weather = Cuacha Terang)
Win = Menang
Wrong = Salah

Peace = Selamat, Peng Ann

(Gloomy Weather = Cuacha Gelap)
Lose = Ilang
Right = Betol

Glossary

Anak-anak = Children
Anjing = Dog
Ari = Day, Ari ni = Today
Beli = Buy
Belok = Turn
Harta = Property (there is no actual word for treasure in Baba)
Jalan = Walk or Road (Always see the context)
Lepair = After
Makanan = Food
Menjela = Window
Pakay = Wear
Pantai/Pantay = Beach
Pasair = Because
Pereksa = Test
Pintu = Door
Pusing = Turn around
Tinggair = Live

Kita suka Chakapan Baba.

Sample Sentences

Ari ni cuacha terang; kita boleh pi pantai.
Today the weather is good; we can go to the beach.

Eh, chelaka! Gua bekin kueh tak sedap. Tawair sekali!
Oh dear! The cakes I made are not tasty. Very tasteless!

Tu gua mia chekgu. Dia orang rajin.
That is my teacher. He is hard-working.

Gua mia rumah selalu semak, kotor. Mesti beli penyapu.
My house is always messy, and dirty. Must buy a broom.

Besok, dia ada pereksa. Tapi dia lupa belajair.
Tomorrow, he has a test. But he forgot to study.

Anak-anak Jane sangat baik pasair semua tau adat.
Jane's children are always good because they know the traditions.

Lu pakay apa? Tak seronoh!
What are you wearing? Not becoming!

Belom orang datang, mesti masak manyak makanan. Lepair orang balek, mesti kemair dapor.
Before people come, we must cook a lot of food. After the people return, we must clean the kitchen.

Belok kiri. Pusing kanan. Jalan terus. Ikot Jalan Anjing.
Turn left. Turn around on the right. Walk straight. Follow Jalan Anjing.

Sekarang ada perang kat Aropah.
At the moment there is a war in Europe.

Bukak menjela. Tutop pintu.
Open the windows. Close the door.

Kami tinggair jaoh dari sini.
We live far from here.

My Family = Gua Mia Anak-Beranak

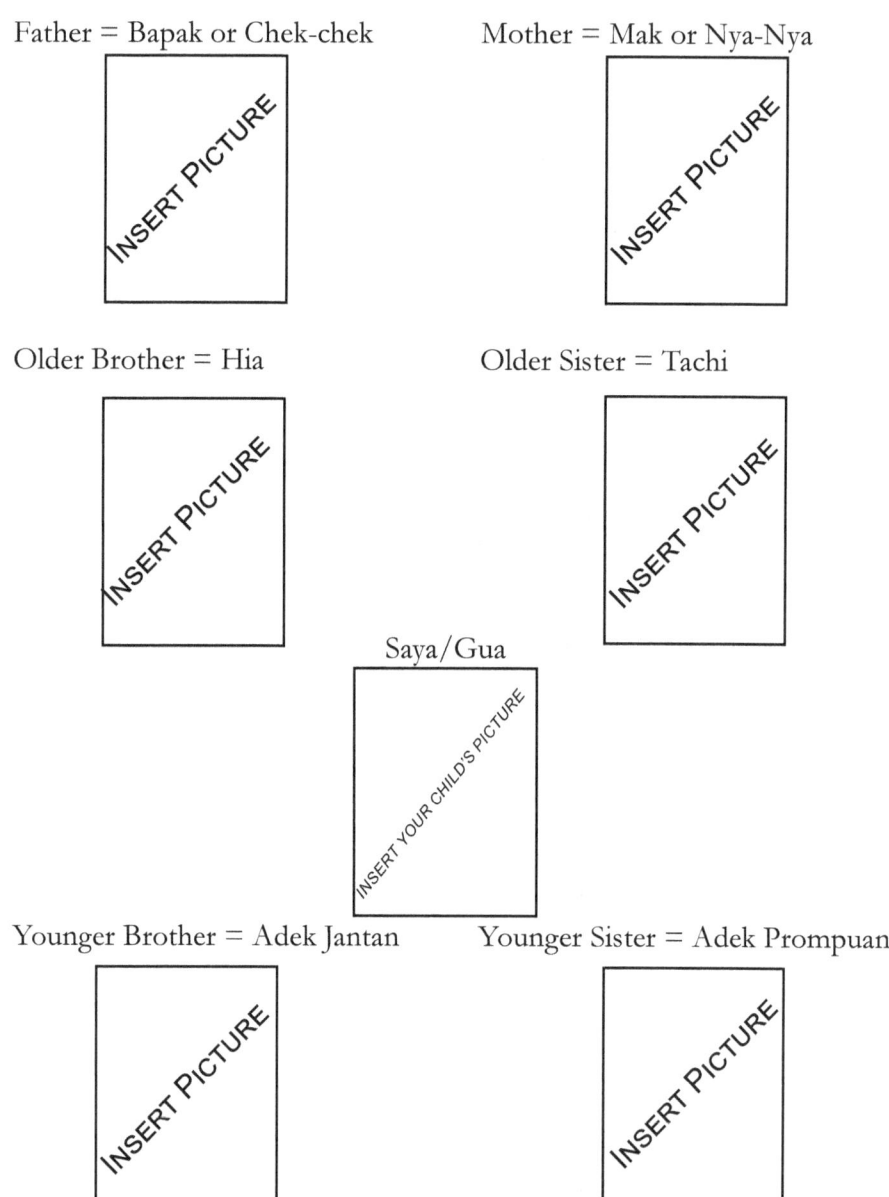

Chakapan Baba lu punya chakapan.

My Cousins = Gua Mia Piau

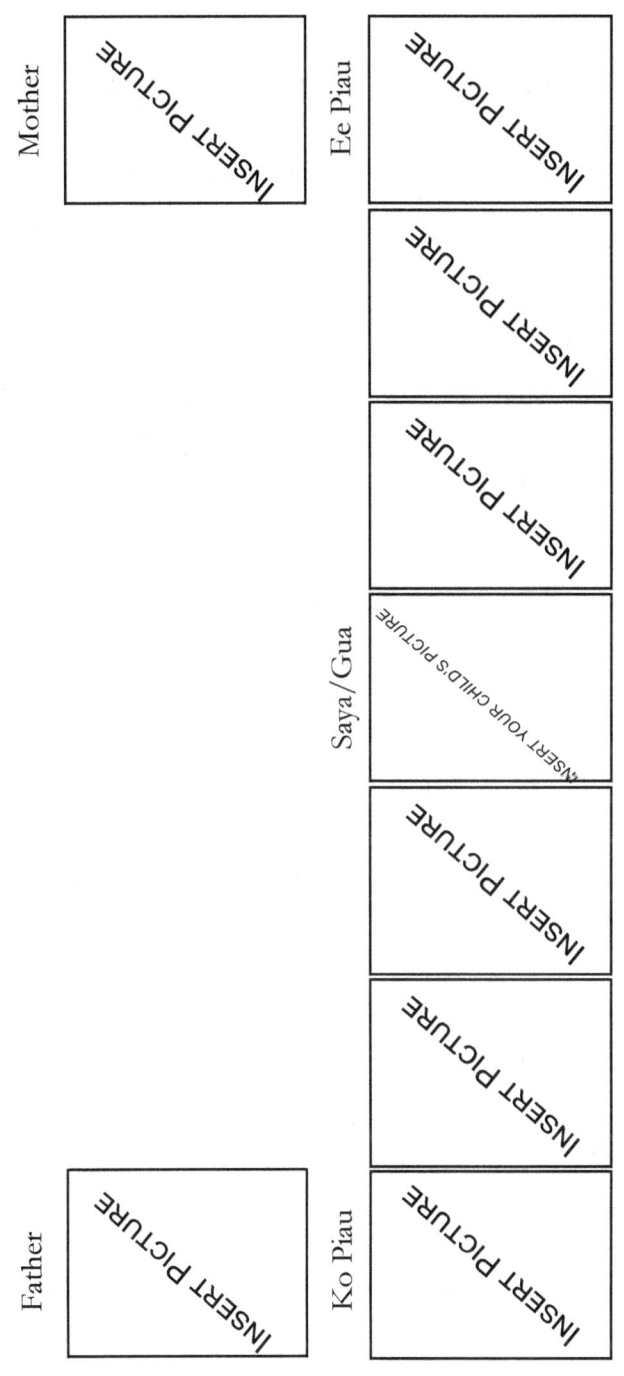

My cousins on my father's side are my Ko Piau while my cousins on my mother's side are my Ee Piau.

Baba Malay is your language.

My Uncles and Aunts = Pangkat Sedara

FATHER

Father's Older Brother = Tua Pek   Father's Older Sister = Mak Ko

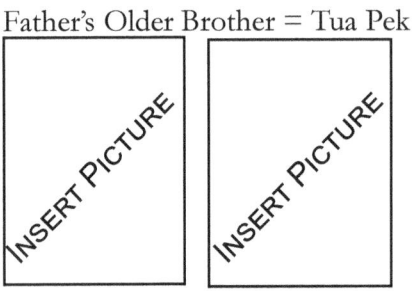

Tua Pek's wife is my Tua Mm   Mak Ko's husband is my Ng/Ko Tio

My Father/Gua mia Bapak

Father's Younger Brother = Ng Chek   Father's Younger Sister = Ko Ko

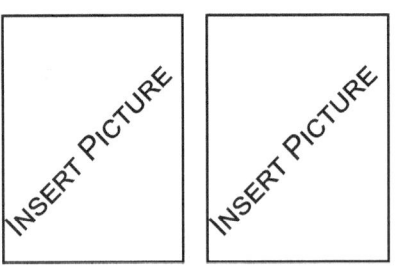 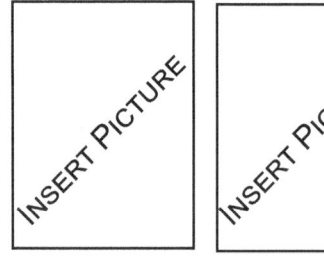

Ng Chek's wife is my Ng Chim   Ko Ko's husband is my Ng/Ko Tio

Kita sayang Chakapan Baba.

My Uncles and Aunts = Pangkat Sedara

MOTHER

Mother's Older Brother = Tua Ku   Mother's Older Sister = Mak Ee

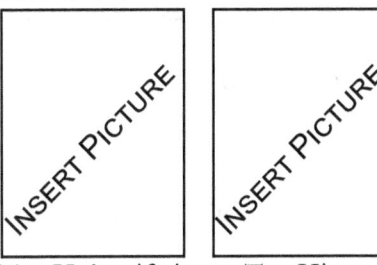 

Tua Ku's wife is my Tua Kim   Mak Ee's husband is my Ng Tio

My Mother/Gua mia Mak

Mother's Younger Brother = Ng Ku   Mother's younger sister = Ee Ee

Ng Ku's wife is my Ng Kim   Ee Ee's husband is my Ng Tio

My Grandparents = Pangkat Sedara

FATHER

Great-Great-Great
Grandfather = Kong Cho Cho Cho

Great-Great-Great
Grandmother = Mak Cho Cho Cho

Great-Great
Grandfather = Kong Cho Cho

Great-Great
Grandmother = Mak Cho Cho

Great-
Grandfather = Kong Cho

Great
Grandmother = Mak Cho

Grandfather = Kong Kong
or Lai Kong

Grandmother = Ma Ma
or Lai Ma

[INSERT PICTURE]

[INSERT PICTURE]

My Father

[INSERT PICTURE]

Gua/Saya

[INSERT YOUR CHILD'S PICTURE]

To try Baba Malay.

My Grandparents = Pangkat Sedara

MOTHER

Great-Great-Great
Grandfather = Kong Cho Cho Cho

Great-Great
Grandfather = Kong Cho Cho

Great-
Grandfather = Kong Cho

Grandfather = Kong Kong
      or Gua Kong

Great-Great-Great
Grandmother = Mak Cho Cho Cho

Great-Great
Grandmother = Mak Cho Cho

Great
Grandmother = Mak Cho

Grandmother = Ma Ma
      or Gua Ma

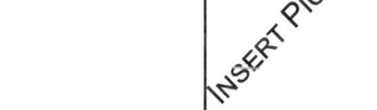

My Mother

Gua/Saya

Chobak Chakapan Baba.

Extended Family Terminology

Ancestors
    Ancestors of 3 generations ago - Nenek Moyang
    Ancestors of 4 generations ago - Moyang

Brother
    Brother-in-law - Chau
    Elder Brother - Hia or Ng Ko
    Father's Eldest Brother - Tua Pek
    Father's Elder Brother - Ng Pek
    Younger Brother - Adek or Adek Jantan
Father's Younger Brother - Ng Chek
    Younger Brother - Adek
Child - Anak
    (Eldest) - Anak Sulong
    (Last or Youngest) - Anak Cuchi Perot
    (Only) - Anak Tunggal
    (Youngest) - Anak Bongsu
Daughter - Anak Prompuan
    Daughter-in-law - Menantu
Family Members - Anak-beranak
Father - Bapak or Chek-chek
    Father's Eldest Brother - Tua Pek
    Father's Elder Brother - Ng Pek
    Father's Elder Sister - Mak Ko
    Father-in-law - Ng Kua
    Father's Younger Brother - Ng Chek
    Father's Younger Sister - Ko Ko

Grandchild - Chu-chu (Singular or Plural)
    Great-grandchild - Chik-chik
    Great-great-grandchild - Oneng-oneng
    Great-great-grandchild - Kueh Wajek

Grandfather - Kong Kong
    Grandfather on your father's side - Lai Kong
    Grandfather on your mother's side - Gua Kong
    Great-grandfather - Kong Cho
    Great-great-grandfather - Kong Cho Cho
    Great-great-great- grandfather - Kong Cho Cho Cho

Grandmother - Ma ma
    Grandmother on your father's side - Lai Ma
    Grandmother on your mother's side - Gua Ma
    Great-grandmother - Mak Cho
    Great-great-grandmother - Mak Cho Cho
    Great-great-great-grandmother - Mak Cho Cho Cho

Husband - Laki

Mother - Mak or Nya-nya
    Mother's Eldest Brother - Tua Ku
    Mother's Elder Brother - Ng Ku
    Mother's Eldest Sister - Mak Ee or Tua Ee
    Mother's Elder Sister - Jee Ee
    Mother-in-law - Nio
    Mother's Younger Brother - Ng Ku
    Mother's Younger Sister - Ee Ee

Son   - Anak Jantan
    Son-in-law - Kia Sai

Sibling - Adek-beradek
Sister
    Elder Sister - Tachi
    Elder Sister-in-law - Ng So or Toa So
    Father's Elder Sister - Mak Ko
    Father's Younger Sister - Ko Ko
    Younger Sister - Adek or Adek Prompuan
    Younger Sister-in-law - Adek

Wife   - Bini

Lu mo belajair Baba Malay.

NOTES

Baba Malay or Chakapan Baba or the Baba language was born when Chinese traders sailed down to Southeast Asia and intermarried with the local women. A mix of Hokkien and Malay, Baba Malay went into decline after WWII as many Peranakans were killed.

This is the reason why there are no Baba Malay equivalent to some words today. When in doubt English words are often used.

Another reason is language assimilation.

There are also two registers to Baba Malay:

    1. Alus i.e., a refined form that women tended to speak.
    2. Kasair i.e., a coarser version practised by men.

Baba Malay tended to be spoken rather than written so there are many variations in the spelling e.g.,

    kreja or kerja (work)

When in doubt I referred to Kenneth Chan's *Baba Malay For Everyone - A comprehensive guide to the Peranakan language* as well as William Gwee Thian Hock's *A Baba Malay Dictionary.*

Baba Malay is also sadly considered an endangered language.

Let's do our best to change this!

Bibek Theresa

About the Author

Theresa Fuller

Theresa Fuller has always loved stories and story-telling, but it was not until the birth of her first son that she became a full-time writer. Her aim was to write stories about her culture: Southeast Asia.

Theresa was Head of Computing at various private schools in Sydney. She has also been a Higher School Certificate (HSC) Examiner and HSC Assessor. Her teaching degrees have seen her work in primary and secondary schools and at Kalgoorlie College in Western Australia.

Her first published novel in 2018 was *THE GHOST ENGINE*, a steampunk fantasy about the fictitious granddaughter of Ada Lovelace, the world's first programmer. Theresa has published books on Southeast Asian mythology: *THE GIRL WHO BECAME A GODDESS* (2019), *THE GIRL SUDAN PAINTED LIKE A GOLD RING* (2022) and *EATING THE LIVER OF THE EARTH* - collection of the lost folktales of the mousedeer Sang Kanchel.

In 2023, *WHERE CRANES WEAVE AND BAMBOO SINGS* a visual narrative textbook for children and beginner writers was published.

In 2020, Theresa lost many family members. She threw heself into researching her family history as a way to deal with her grief. This was when she discovered that the language of her ancestors - Baba Malay - was on the verge of extinction. As a writer, teacher and selfpublishing author, Theresa found herself in an unusual position - she was able to create the curriculum that was needed to help fill a vacuum.

The result is the **Baba Malay Today** series. And now the **New Peranakan Tales** series starting with GUA PI KEDAY.

All in aid of saving the language.

www.theresafuller.com

Thank you for your support!

More Books in the Baba Malay Today Series

Book 1 - Interrogatory Part I SAPA, APA, MANA or
WHO, WHAT, WHERE

Book 2 - Interrogatory Part II AMCHAM, APASAIR, BILA or
HOW, WHY, WHEN

Book 3 - Conjunctions TAPI, ABIS, PASAIR or
BUT, SO, BECAUSE

Book 4 - Prepositions ATAIR, KAT, BAWAH or
TOP, NEAR, BOTTOM

Book 5 - Antonyms ALUS, KA, KASAR or
DELICATE, OR, COARSE

Book 6 - Essence CHAKAPAN BABA ATI or
THE HEART OF BABA MALAY

Book 7 - Poetry CHAKAPAN BABA PANTON or
BABA MALAY POETRY

Book 8 - Idioms CHAKAPAN BABA CHAKAPAN or
BABA MALAY IDIOMS

Dear Reader,

Thank you for the purchase of this book.

Please help us spread the word as we try to save our language.

Bibek Theresa

Sydney, 18th of June, 2022

Jangan lupa Chakapan Baba.

www.ingramcontent.com/pod-product-compliance
Lightning Source LLC
Chambersburg PA
CBHW070341120526
44590CB00017B/2980